LOVING MESSAGES
FROM MY SON AND THE ANGELS

Written and illustrated by

Ruthe Ann Walsh

Foreword by Regina Rosenthal PT, MA, RYT-200

To bring comfort, peace and reassurance to anyone grieving a loss or wondering if there is an afterlife.

This book includes healing artwork infused with Reiki and intuitive or channeled art.

b

c

Table of Contents

Dedication

This book is dedicated to my son, William John Walsh. He passed away at the age of 41 on August 11th, 2018 after a year-long battle with brain cancer.

Part of his obituary that his father wrote:

"He loved the outdoors; he was an avid mountain biker and snowboarder. Bill also loved the beach where he spent many hours a day. He was a great guy who always had something clever to say, followed by one of his winning smiles. He was helpful and caring to people around him."

He was an amazing father to Dylan who was only 13 when Billy was diagnosed. He was a loving son, brother and fiancé.

He taught us how to live with his adventurous ways and how to die, being loving to the end.

We will love you always.

Foreword

I first met Ruthe Ann Walsh at a Cancer Support Community (CSC) program, *Acupressure for Self-Care* that I presented. There was something about Ruthe Ann that I wanted to get to know, something about her quiet yet solid, strong presence that I wanted to understand and connect with more deeply. As group members spoke during that session, Ruthe Ann spoke gently, from a heart-centered place, sharing that she and her husband had lost their 41-year-old son William ("Billy" she called him) to brain cancer on August 11th, 2018. Their 13-year-old grandson, Dylan, had lost his father, and Billy's brother Evan, fiancé Laura and Dylan's mom Janette had also experienced this unfathomable loss.

As I listened to Ruthe Ann speak, I wondered how it was possible for this human being, wife, mother, and grandmother to continue and remain present in such a grounded and heart-centered way after the unimaginable loss of a child. How was she able to do this? Who or what supported and sustained her? What tools had she discovered? How had she kept her heart open after such a devastating loss?

My life journey included learning and practicing yoga, meditation, complementary medicine, healing touch modalities, Chinese medicine and acupressure, the chakra system, qigong, and spirituality as ways of thinking about life and our purpose and mission here. In my early thirties the birth of our first child, after two miscarriages, brought insight and sacred moments when I understood and sensed the miraculous nature of life and love. These moments changed me and how I viewed life. Meeting Ruthe Ann also brought moments when this realization deepened. Like Ruthe Ann, I questioned life purpose and life after death when I faced significant challenges and the passing of my mother and friends. During sessions when Billy spoke with Ruthe Ann (while I was present), I was again reminded that love and energy do not stop after we or someone we love passes. I had learned and experienced this by studying and practicing energy medicine.

As a physical therapist, I had worked in hospice and oncology for years prior to meeting Ruthe Ann. I was now working with individuals living with chronic and life-threatening health conditions. I had a sense that what Ruthe Ann was experiencing could support and comfort others, impacted by cancer and/or dealing with grief after the loss of a loved one or facing their own mortality. One day I asked Ruthe Ann if she had considered writing a book about her experiences with Billy to share with others. She knew about the book I had written, with a similar intention of it serving others, and this opened up a whole conversation between us. I'm sure Billy, the Angels, and spirit guides were cheering us on!

During the year, months, and weeks the CSC monthly group met pre covid, Ruthe Ann attended group and individual acupressure sessions with me. I felt honored and in awe each time Ruthe Ann shared highlights from her journey before and since Billy had passed. She still felt his presence, heard his laughter, and was continuously receiving what she described as "messages" from Billy, the Angels, and other spirit guides. She also spoke about healing artwork and movement that came forth after messages received during these love-filled connections.

Early on I didn't know Ruthe Ann had been an art teacher, was a very gifted artist, student of Reiki, and a spiritual seeker. I got to experience her artistry, and the work she brought to the CSC through an art workshop sponsored by the Monmouth Art Museum. Several of the paintings were exhibited during this workshop. What I did know and experience with her, during our sessions, was Billy's continual loving presence and strong desire to speak with Ruthe Ann from what has been called "the other side." Although I had never met Billy, when I indirectly asked her something about Billy during our sessions she would say, "That is so what Billy would say or do."

Billy spoke to Ruthe Ann about living and dying. He told her how significant each moment was, during his passing, when she brought love from her heart to his and perhaps unknowingly midwifed his passing. Billy emphasized again and again the essential need to remember that love and life are miracles and love connects us all. Chinese medicine principles speak about our being the bridge between heaven and earth. Billy told Ruthe Ann "As above so below." Billy spoke about how our gifts and talents can serve others, and bring love and healing into our world and the New Earth. He said he would continue to speak with her about all of this, showing how love is always possible. Billy emphasized that meditation, as a practice, helps connect us with the angels and our spirit guides. However, we MUST remember to ask for help and guidance, followed by listening and trusting… by being open and not attached to the outcome. One theme stood out each time Billy communicated with Ruthe Ann… *Love never dies.*

During the pandemic, and in current times, we are all looking for and needing comfort, peace, and reassurance. Ruthe Ann's book provides this again and again through the energy, love, and spiritual insights and guidance she shares from Billy and the Angels. The beautiful artwork on these pages can provide insights and guidance while sitting quietly with them, asking for support, setting an intention prior, and trusting what arises in your awareness and from your heart.

As I slowly read each page of the manuscript Ruthe Ann sent me and looked meditatively at each painting, it felt like Light emerged from them, surrounding and enfolding me. These were unanticipated and powerful experiences; they brought understanding and insights I hadn't considered prior about love, loss, grief, relationships, compassion, forgiveness, life, death and dying, and miracles available to all of us whenever love and Light touches and connects us to our deepest Self and each other. The beautiful words and Reiki-infused artwork you hold in your hands is a gift from Ruthe Ann, Billy, and the Angels. It is meant to provide insights, comfort, and support for each reader. May the sacred moments you spend with this gift remind you how much you are loved and how significant you/we all are in bringing much-needed healing, Light, and love into our world.

Namaste,

Regina Rosenthal, PT, MA, RYT-200

Introduction

This book is being written because the Angels gave me a clear message to write it, I was not always getting messages from them (that I knew of anyway). When our son Billy got diagnosed with brain cancer, our world fell apart. It made me so mad I wanted to scream. I was mad at God and I felt like the Angels had deserted me.

I thought I knew what grief felt like before. There was a lot of sadness and grief I went through when my grandparents and parents passed, but this was a whole new level. It did not seem like it was anything I could get through. If I started to feel normal, after a while my heart would start to scream out. It was hard getting out of bed, do anything or think of anything else. I felt as if I desperately needed to know what happened to him. Was there life after death? I thought that there was. I had to find out. I knew there were people who could commutate with spirits who passed on. Could I learn to do that? I had to try — I had to know that Billy was alright.

So I started reading books and meeting helpful people. I took a class on learning how to become a medium. At a holistic festival I met a woman who showed me how I could connect with Billy through meditation and readings. At the end of the book you'll find information on the books and people who can help — I have met so many who are grieving and I would love to be of some comfort to them if I can.

At first I was finally getting 'yes' and 'no' answers with automatic writing. Then one day it just took off. It was so wonderful to be getting answers — like a miracle, and best of all I knew it was true. That beautiful Light was my son and it did not go out. Energy does not stop, but it changes form. I now have over six journals full of loving messages; I have only included some.

It was such a wonderful surprise being able to do this, but was I only able to do it with my son? Then, over time, I got more messages from different spirits — an amazing surprise every time.

I received so many beautiful messages; they are too beautiful not to share with those who may benefit from them. The book starts with channeled messages I received from Angels who told me they were my muses. I didn't know how to write a book but I was not going to argue with them. It seemed as if the messages from Billy should come first, then the channeled information from the Angels. Also, included is artwork from when I started getting the messages — there are symbols and a heart that evolved over time. The paintings are all channeled art or intuitive images. I will explain each one at the end of the book.

I hope this book brings you peace and comfort. If you feel it is in conflict with what you believe, then it is not for you. The book is not meant to offend anyone — you will see that the Angels mention this as well.

Messages From Billy

It took some time before I could master the automatic writing. I was getting little messages, like the time I was thinking about jumping into a pool but the water was too cold — he was telling me to go for it and I jumped in. There were others like that. Then I had one wonderful visitation dream where he was telling me everything would be alright and that he was still there for me.

As mentioned earlier, this journey started out with getting answers for 'yes' and 'no' questions. Then at that holistic event I had a session with Brigitte Boyea; she is at The Light Bridge Center for Transformation. The first time I met with her she gave me a message: Billy was so sorry. At first I did not understand why he was saying that, but he was sorry for all the sadness and heartache his death caused. After that first time, I was getting more communication from him. In the second session, Brigitte was very helpful advising me on how to connect with my son. This time his message was that he had to die when he did, that it was in the contract, part of the plan… that it had to be that way and that he has work to do now. He wanted to work with me making healing artwork. The first channeled painting we did was the heart with one rose and a rosebud. The second was the spirals. At first, I was worried that I could not do art that heals, then I relaxed and did what I was called to do. I realized all art can be a healing tool for the person creating it and hopefully the person viewing it, if that is the intention.

Later during a Seva Stress Release session with Regina Rosenthal, Billy popped in. She asked me what I do when I'm stressed and Billy came in (Regina was getting this) and said I should shake it off. Regina laughed; she could see what he was doing. He was moving like one of those plastic figures in front of a car dealership. Billy never lost his sense of humor.

Then, she talked about how caring and loving he is and she heard him say, "Okay, let's not get carried away." That was so Billy.

After that, it was like the flood gates opened and it was much easier to hear him. Besides the writing, Billy started adding movement during communication. It was a combination of dance, yoga, Tai Chi and Qi Gong. The beautiful movement first, and then we would write.

His first messages were repeated a lot and have been carried through all of the journals.

We are all connected in Love. Everything is Love. We are all Love.

Flow in Love and Let Go of Worry.

First channeled painting with Billy, Heart with Rose and Rose Bud.

Then he would sign and write

Love

Billy

And the infinity sign ∞

The heart with the rose, which you will see, changed over time.

Dear Billy   *9/2/19*

Me: Love you.

Billy: Love you too.

Me: What does the spiral mean?

Billy: What goes around comes around and all goes back to the beginning.

Me: Beautiful!! Thank you. Are there angels there? Can I talk to them?

Billy: Yes.

Me: Do you have jobs to do?

Billy: Yes, watching over you and others.

Me: How can I help?

Billy: Pray for me

Me: Should I go to church?

Billy: Yes, any plain old church will do.

Second channeled painting with Billy, Gold and Copper Spirals

Dear Billy   *10/7/19*

Me: Happy Birthday my sweet boy!!!

Miss you—You would be 43 today.

Billy: Love You. Flow in love, the universe loves you.

Me: Thank you. Love you sweetheart. Are you happy?

Billy: Yes.

Me: Good, I'm happier this year on 10/7 than last year because of all the connections with you. YOU SAVED ME!

Hello Billy   *11/6/19*

Me: I will try my best to keep Dylan and Evan safe. Can you help on this trip to Aruba?

Billy: Yes.

Me: Can the whole spirit team help? And send healing?

Billy: Yes.

Me: Will your father be OK?

Billy: Yes!

Me: Thank you! Love you, see you there!

Hello Billy   *11/11/19*

I love you. Were you with us in Aruba? I felt that you were.

Billy: Yes!

Me: When?

Billy: We went snorkeling.

Me: Did you see Dylan jumping off the boat?

Billy: Yes.

Me: You must be proud, he is so much like you.

Billy: Yes he is.

Me: Did you jump with him?

Billy: Yes.

Me: How about the horseback riding—he liked that the most.

Billy: Yes, I was right behind him.

Me: I'm so glad. I knew that you would keep him safe.

Billy: Of course.

Me: Did you help us find the sea glass and heart shapes?

Billy: The blue one.

Me: That was so beautiful, the best one we found—thank you.

Billy: Welcome–the heart shapes also.

Me: Thank you. Love it all.

Me: What was your favorite part of the trip?

Billy: Loving you all. Thank you for taking D.

Me: We love him so much.

Billy: Me too

Me: ∞ *I brought a necklace with this sign in Aruba.*

Billy: I know.

Me: The money in the pocket was a nice surprise for D.

Billy: I put it there.

Me: Thank you. The light in the kitchen that goes off and on—is that you?

Billy: Yes.

Me: Love you.

Billy: Love you too.

Dear Billy   *11/16/19*

Me: What are you doing?

Billy: Flowing in Love. You can do this in meditation. Just close your eyes and imagine. You are floating in water on a perfect day. Let your worries float away.

Me: That is beautiful, thank you.

Me: Did I not send enough love to you to heal?

Billy: We could not stop it, it had to be. Sorry, Mom

Me: I wish it didn't happen and I could have helped.

Billy: We tried.

Me: Yes we did, all of us loving you.

Billy: We will be okay. Send light and love.

Me: What else?

Billy: Love, only love. We are here.

Me: Thank you. Love you and our spirit team.

Hello Billy,   *11/17/19*

Me: What is my lesson for today?

Billy: Love all always!

Me: Are you in a different place now? Did you evolve more?

Billy: Yes.

Me: What is it like there?

Billy: Floating in space.

(Meditated and went floating with Billy)

Me: Flowing in love.

Billy: You can do this in meditation. Just close your eyes and imagine you are floating in space.

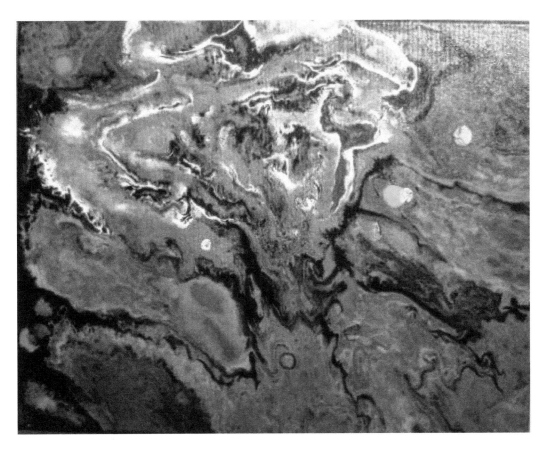

Floating in Space

(Meditated and went floating with Billy)

Me: That was so beautiful—flowing with you—freeing—healing

Loving. Thank you, Love You, Mom

Billy: Love you!

Billy

(He drew a large infinity sign)

Me: Love this sign—love never ends—the spirit never ends.

In another letter, I asked the spirit team (Angels, spirit guides, soul family: my parents, grandparents, and my aunt to please send healing. They said: We work on it always. We try to help. We can do just so much. We can help if you pray to the Angels.

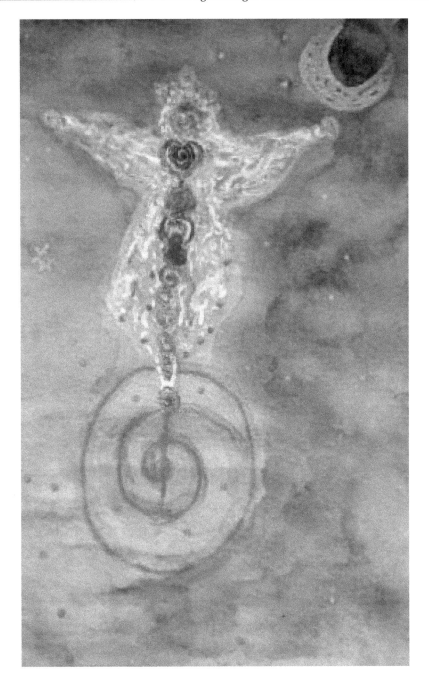

Beautiful Spirit in the Sky, the Spirit is sending love to all.

Me: Who hears our prayers?

The spirit team said, "We all do, so pray. You are blessed. We all love you. Don't be mad at God, it had to be. See you soon."

Me: Hope not too soon.

They said, "No, live your life. We are here. Love to all."

Dear Billy,   *12/20/19*

Me: Do you celebrate Christmas there?

Billy: Yes.

Me: Merry Christmas! What do they do?

Billy: A lot of singing and dancing, and visits with our loved ones sending love. A lot of lights, the whole planet lights up.

Me: Beautiful!

Billy: It is. Love to all!

Northern Lights

When I ask about cures, the answer is always love.

Me: What is the best healing method?

Billy: Love! Love is the cure.

Hi Billy,   *12/31/19*

Me: It's New Year's Eve–tomorrow will be 2020—hope it is a good year. Do you celebrate it there?

Billy: No, not really. We don't have the time. You are getting better at flowing in love. You are loved by many. When you are sad, we are always here loving you.

Me: Thank you. You saved me. Were we together in another life? Is reincarnation real?

Billy: Yes, we will all be together again.

Me: Were you my son?

Billy: No, we were friends!

Me: What should I be doing?

Billy: Praying, flowing, learning, practicing Reiki and art therapy.

Me: Thank you, love you.

(Asking the Angels about healing)

Me: Do you help with healing?

Billy: Yes we can but only so much.

Me: Are there cures for Parkinson's and cancer?

Billy: Yes but the Archangels do the bigger things. We help with smaller things, like connecting the right people.

Love to All ∞ *and drawing of the heart with one rose inside.*

Dear Billy,   *6/21/20*

Me: Happy Father's Day. You are the best father—love you. I wished your father a happy Father's Day and he said he's not happy. He misses you so much, as we all do. Maybe for Father's Day you could somehow show him that you are still here. Can you do that?

Billy: Yes!

Me: Wonderful—thank you. What can I do for you?

Billy: Paint, pray, heal, love, be happy.

Me: Thank you – I will try, I will.

Billy: The best is yet to come.

Me: Love you!

Billy: Love you too.

He drew with me a beautiful rose with one bud inside the heart.

Dear Billy,   *7/6/20*

Me: Thank you. Thank you to all! Your father's test came back; no new tumors.

(We drew a page of hearts and roses)

Me: So he is cancer-free?

Billy: Yes!

Me: Thank you, love you.

Billy: LOVE YOU.

Me: What did you do today?

Billy: I was there with the doctor. He is a good doctor; he prays when he works on people. I watched over you and Dad.

Me: Love You!

Billy: Love you too.   (We both drew a large infinity sign)

Hi Billy

Me: Think of you so much. Your angel date is coming up, Aug.11.

Billy: Yes 2 yr.

Me: Sometimes it feels like yesterday and other times it seems so long ago.

Billy: Love you.

Me: Love you, my sweet boy. Austin is such a good friend. Were you there when he took Dylan golfing?

Billy: Yes, he did good, love him so and Austin is great.

Me: When this virus is over, is that when we have the New Earth?

Billy: Yes, it will start then.

Me: What do you think I should or will do?

Billy: Pray, love and heal. Your artwork will help. We need to work on it.

Me: Love that you are with me, I'm so lucky. People may think I'm crazy if I tell them.

Billy: Yes, but you should, they will all know someday.

Into the Void – Intuitive painting from a meditation

Dear Billy,   7/27/20

Me: Hi honey, how are you?

Billy: You are in the right place. You are on the right track, just keep going. You will get there.

Me: Where?

Billy: You are evolving, you are coming home. You can see better what has to be done. We are working on it. Will you help?

Me: Yes, what should I do?

Billy: You are going to walk the walk of the knowing. You are going to be with us here so get ready. It will be okay, you are going to work there with us here.

Me: How will that work?

Billy: We will tell you how when you are ready.

Me: Can I travel there in my dreams to learn? But I need to remember my dreams.

Billy: Yes, you will. You will get ready.

Me: What can I do to get ready?

Billy: You should meditate and connect with us more. We are here for you.

Intuitive Image Number One started with one continuous line, which turned out to be a mother and child with an infinity sign connecting them. What it wants to be is always a surprise.

Intuitive Image Number Two

Me: Thank you—I love you.

Billy: We love you, we will help, it will be ok.

Me: Told your father that you try to talk to him.

Billy: I do but he doesn't hear me.

Me: He misses you so much.

Billy: I know, I hear him, I love him, he needs to believe in this.

Me: How can we get him to?

Billy: He will someday.

There is so much that I need to leave some out. He talks about his son Dylan often and that I need to do artwork.

One day I asked, "Are miracles real?"

He said, "Yes they happen all the time in small ways. Life is a miracle, your art is a miracle. Love is the biggest one of all."

Dear Billy,   *12/7/20*

Me: How are you?

Billy: Good and you?

Me: Good, what info do you have for me today?

Billy: Love, Flow and Pray. I know that you are doing that and that is good. Love everything and everyone. We are all made from love. Flow in love and you will be connected to the Divine, me and all that is. Pray for the Earth.

Me: When will Covid-19 go away?

Billy: We are still working on it, but soon.

Me: What about the vaccine, will it work?

Billy: Yes, it will work.

The Lavender Couple… Do you see what I see?

Dear Billy,   *12/20/20*

Me: The crystal bowls are so beautiful, my body moves in a way that makes me think there are words to the music but I don't know what they are.

Billy: Yes, it is saying you are love, you are here for a reason. You are love. Love is all there is.

Me: Lovely, what a beautiful song.

Billy: You are on the right path. You are doing your work.

Me: Is the book the first thing I should be doing?

Billy: Yes, it is then the cards, then the retreat. You know all you need to know now.

Me: Love to ∞

Love ∞

Billy

Another time after listening to the crystal bowls I asked him what they were saying. And this is what he said, "They are saying you are light and love, remember that always. They want people to remember to always come home to that knowing. Everything is love for everyone. It is filling you up with love."

Dear Billy,

Me: How are you?

Billy: OK and you?

Me: Good, what have you been up to?

Billy: Just hanging out with the Spirits and Angels. We are working on the Covid-19.

Me: How is that going?

Billy: OK, but people are not listening so it takes longer.

Me: Will the vaccine work?

Billy: Yes!

Me: Will it cause health problems?

Billy: Some but it is needed.

Me: Should your father and I get it?

Billy: Yes!

Billy: We are going to be together again soon. We will have other lives. So please don't be so sad. I will be with you. I love you.

Dear Billy   *3/12/21*

Me: How are you?

Billy: Good – you are doing good, keep it up.

Me: Thank you, I need to write the intro for the book and would like to include some of your messages.

Billy: You should say all that you are called to say. It will help others know about life after death. You could tell them how to communicate with us. They first should meditate, then ask, then listen, write it down or let the pen move.

Dear Billy   *4/7/21*

Me: Thanks for the healing, feeling better now.

Billy: You need to do the work. You will grow. Much love to you. You are here to write the book, do the artwork for it and love.

Billy: You are doing a good job—don't worry about it.

Me: What about the New Earth?

Billy: The New Earth is the dream of many, it can come when people start to care more about each other. And when they start to take better care of our Mother Earth. Since we are all connected, and love is what it is all about, if we bring more love into our hearts then the whole planet will feel that and then we will head into the New Earth. Many are resistant, so it will take some time.

Me: What will the New Earth be like?

Billy: It will be more like it is here. So as above as below. It will not be totally the same but closer.

Me: What else do you want to say?

Billy: Love really is the most important thing, so love everyone and everything.

Me: You were not a religious person when you were here. Do you regret that now?

Billy: Yes, if I was then maybe I would have understood more. And the going, the leaving would have been easier. You don't have to go to church if that is not your thing. You just need to tune in—the way you do now.

Me: Thank you that is good information for people to know. Anything else?

Billy: I want to let people know that there is an afterlife that they do go on —it is different but not the end. And just love, love, love and trust.

Me: That is such a comfort for me and I hope for others. You are a blessing to me.

Billy: You are a blessing to me. Thank you.

Me: Love you!

Billy: Love you too.

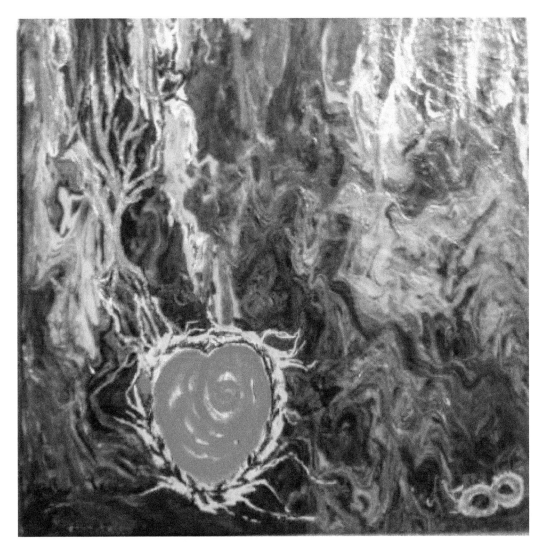

Heart of the Mystic Forest.

The Listening Tree with Wise Owl. Do you see the ear that just appeared there?

Channeled from My Spirit Team… Divine blueprint, everything is energy.

My Secret Garden… A vision from a meditation

Answers from the Angels

What is spirituality?

It is a way of thinking about life, the Universe and why we are here.

Wonderful, tell me more, please.

You come to this world with a mission: your purpose. And you are never alone. Others come with you. You may meet them later in your life for the reason they are here to help you with. Or they may be your parents, or sister or brother. We all have a purpose for being here. You are part of it as they are part of their reason for coming to earth at this time. You also have other people that you will help on their journeys.

Your job is to find out what your purpose is. Look at what you are good at and find a way to be of service or helping others using your special abilities. Find your bliss, what you love, what brings you joy.

If you like music, find your song and sing it for all to hear. If it is art, draw, paint, any type of art. Art can be your medicine. When you find it, share it.

Your purpose can be teaching, bringing people together, building things, or farming. Whatever it is, do your best and it will be wonderful.

Please tell us more about never being alone.

You are with angels, who are here to help you if you ask them to. They can comfort you and let you know if you are on the right path by sending you signs, like feathers, pennies and numbers like 11:11.

They love you. They can also send you a warm feeling that can be just like a hug. Others are here to watch over you. You can have a whole spirit team with spirit guides. One thing to know—you need to ask them for help or guidance, they will not just do something. It's like you are permitting them. There are Archangels you can call on for help with different things. They have things they are best at doing. Archangel Michael is a protector; you can ask him for protection. There are many books written about angels, so you can find out much more about them.

Do not be afraid of Spirits or Angels. Just say that they must be of love and light. They love to help. They can see the bigger picture from where they are.

What are some things they would like us to know?

We are all connected, with the earth and each other. And we all came from stardust, so we are all the same. We are all one.

Everything has a spirit—a rock, tree, the earth, people—everything.

So we should treat everything and everyone with love.

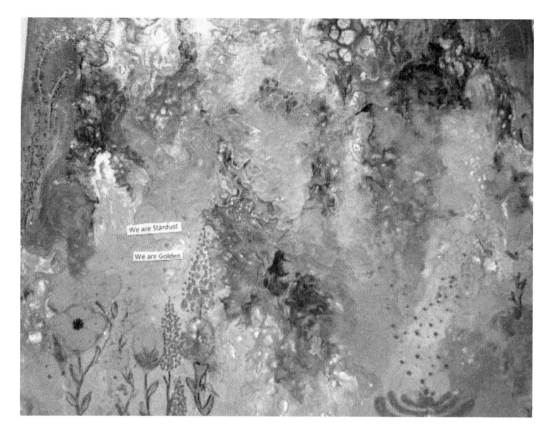

The Garden

This is the next thing they want us to know:

Everything is Love.

It is like the Beatles song, "All you need is Love. Love is all you need."

Love is all that is. God is love.

You may use whatever word you want for God or use the word love.

Different religions have different words and names. But this is not about that, this is all religions, the whole Universe. So God or Love is the creator of all that is, and we are all one, all connected. Then we are all Love or God; that good that is in every one of us.

Why do the angels want me to write this book?

We want you to let people know they are never alone. We can be called on for so many reasons. We can help in so many different ways. In small ways, like finding a parking space, what to wear that day, what is best to eat and so many more; to the bigger ways, like how to live with the loss of a loved one. We can comfort you when you are feeling sad.

Infinite Possibilities, Goddess of the Moon…

We send love and give you an angel hug. We can send the right people to you that you may need at that time. It could be people that you may or may not know, but are the ones you need at that time. We can also help with learning different things that need to be or want to be learned. Sometimes a book you should see will just fall off a shelf for you to pick up. That is us — Your Angels!

Pay attention, we send signs in many ways. Ever just open a book to any page and find something meaningful for you there? Someone may start talking about something you want to know about and they do not know why they just started telling you about it. Answers can even pop up in emails. Maybe there is a word the angels want you to see for an answer to a problem or a question you have. You can go to sleep with a question for the angels and you may get the answer in a dream or you may wake up knowing the answer. Did you ever wake up with a song in your head? Think about the words to the song, does it have some meaning for you?

So when you have a problem you can ask your Angels. No problem is too big or too small for them. The main thing we want you to know is:

We are here for you — ask us for help. It is our job, it is what we want to do. We love you but you do need to give your permission.

Spiritual understanding can unite different religions.

We feel that all religions are correct. We are all one. We, all people, all living things are connected. One person is no better than another one.

Reaching Out, the message was to reach out to make a connection, shine your light to infinity and beyond. From my spirit team.

We are all one within all of the Universe. Everything has a spirit that you can communicate with, like a tree, a rock, or a piece of artwork. You can communicate with mostly anything. It may take some training or practice. The Shamans believe that all things are alive with a spirit. Learning the ways of the Shamans would be helpful.

Humans need to learn to treat the Earth better. You are hurting it with the pollution of the water, soil, and air. Please remember we are all one and that love is what matters. Loving yourself, others and all things.

We care so much about you all. We love you all.

What happens when someone you love dies?

They will lose their physical body, but then their spirit lives on. They will be with their family members that passed before them (their soul family). They will be in a state of flow. They will flow in love. They can come to see you and they will love you more than ever. You may not see them or know that they are there.

But you may feel their love for you. It is like that warm feeling, as we said, that feels like a hug but without touching. They will want you to know that they still love you more than ever and always will.

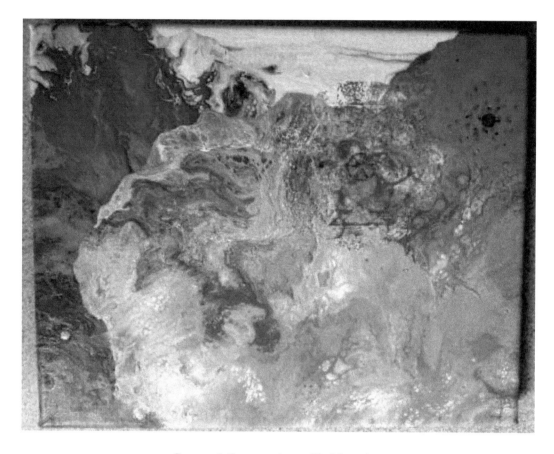

Sacred Geometry with Heart…

You will be with them again when you pass on. So you do not need to be afraid. They will be there to greet you, in a most beautiful place.

This is just one life. We all have many. We are here to do different things in each lifetime.

So, we should live our lives the best we can.

Finding out our purpose is half the fun. So, enjoy all your life.

We will tell you the secret — Love is the most important thing there is in life.

So much Love to you, dear one.

What do You See?

Beautiful Universe

Beyond the Beyond

The New Moon in Taurus, which calls in the Light and Love…

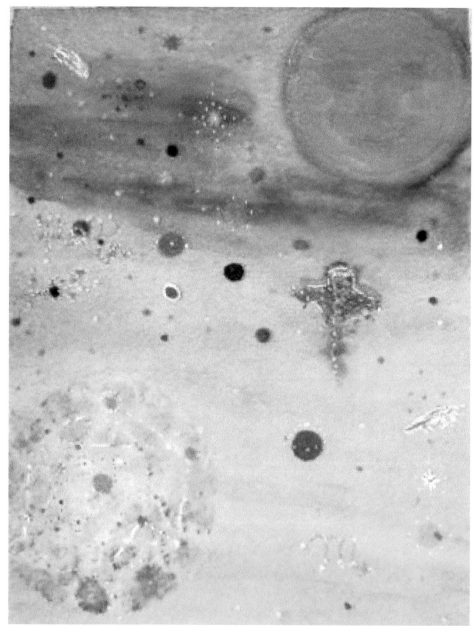

Full Pink Moon in Scorpio – Flow in Love.

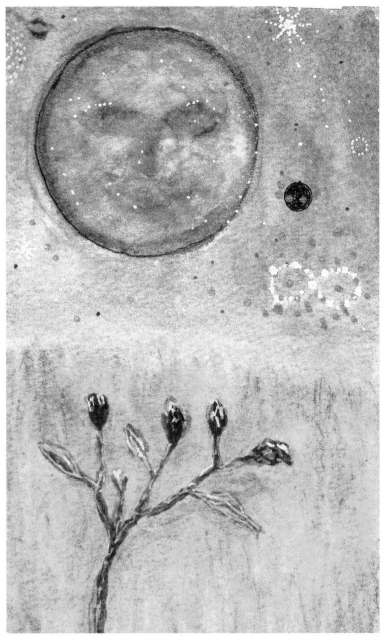

Full Moon in Libra – Libra is for balance and releasing what is out of balance.

Sending Healing to India, 5/21/21, many lives are being lost at this time.

Listing of Artwork

Cover. Heart with Rose—for the cover of the book.

b. Close-up photo of Billy in a collage of sympathy cards.

1. Photo of sympathy card collage

9. Heart with Rose and Rose Bud –channeled painting on canvas 11x14

12. Gold and Copper Spirals –channeled painting on canvas 8x10

17. Floating in Space 11x14 canvas mixed media.

19. Beautiful Spirit in the Sky. This spirit is sending love to all. 2021 7x6 watercolors

21. Northern Lights—mixed media on canvas 11x12

26. Into the Void from a meditation–intuitive painting. The beings seemed to just pop out of the watercolor paint

28. Intuitive Imagery #1, Started with one continuous line. It turned out to be a mother and child with infinity signs connecting them—what it wants to be is always a surprise. Markers 7x9 on pap

29. Intuitive Imagery #2, markers 7x6 on paper.

32. The Lavender Couple 4x5 on canvas board pour painting. Do you see what I see?

37. Heart of the Mystical Forrest—mixed media on canvas 12x12

38. Evolving Heart Drawing

39. My Secret Garden—mixed media on paper 7x6—a vision from a meditation.

40. The Listening Tree with Wise Owl–mixed media on canvas board 8x10 Do you see the ear that just appeared there?

41. Channeled from Spirit team—Divine Blueprint—Everything is energy; thoughts, emotions, etc. 7x6 mixed media

44. The Garden—We are stardust—We are golden—mixed media on canvas 14x11

46. Infinite Possibilities—Goddess of the Moon is in the style of Botticelli's "Birth of Venus" (well kind of). On paper—mixed media 10x12

48. Reaching Out –The message was to reach out to make a connection. Shine your light to infinity and beyond—from my spirit team. 7x6 on paper mixed media.

50. Sacred Geometry with Heart—mixed media on canvas 8x10

52. What do You See? 9x12 mixed media—infinity signs, birds, hearts on canvas

New Moon in Taurus Call in light and love, 6/21/21, mixed media on paper

53. Beautiful Universe (with ½ face moon) 11x14 canvas mixed media

54. Beyond the Beyond, 11x14 canvas mixed media

55. New Moon in Taurus Call in light and love, 6/21/21, mixed media on paper

56. Full Pink Moon in Scorpio Flow is Love mixed media

57. Full Moon in Libra 3/26/21 Libra is for balance and releasing what is out of balance. Mixed media 7x6

58. Sending Healing to India 5/21/21. Many lives were being lost there at this time due to Covid-19. 7x6 mixed media on paper.

Acknowledgments

First I would like to thank my husband Bill. He has helped me with the technology of creating this book and he has loved me through our grief. We have spent 51+ years together.

To Evan, Billy's brother, who misses him so much.

To Dylan, Billy's son, whose heart is broken with the loss of his father. My hope is that reading this book will bring some comfort to all that are grieving.

To Laura, Billy's fiancée, who slept in a chair by his side each night he needed to be in a hospital.

To Billy's close friends Vinny, Austin and DJ, who continue to spend time with Dylan, by taking him snowboarding, golfing, biking and more. Austin has done all the activities with him as well as things like helping him get his part-time job.

To Janette, Dylan's mother, for sharing him with us and for always keeping us up on how he is doing.

To our dance family, for their wonderful meals they sent us with their love. To Gloria for her amazing support with all the professional help when she volunteered all those late nights with such love and kindness to all of us.

To Jan Leeds and all loving and caring friends and family who supported us along the way.

To the people at the Cancer Support Community — Debra McGivney, social worker and teacher Regina Rosenthal (Regina was the first to say that I should write a book), for all the support they gave me after Billy passed.

Regina has been such an amazing mentor and an essential part of the writing of this book.

To Carol Fuchs, for all her help with the making of this book.

And of course, my gratitude to the Muse Angels and my son Billy, for all the messages and channeled artwork. They are the reason for this book.

About the Author

Ruthe Ann was an art teacher who got to work with children of all ages. She enjoyed teaching for many years. After retiring, she took her love of all things from the sea and started making sea glass jewelry which she still makes. The sea glass is collected by her husband and herself, mostly from the beaches of Puerto Rico.

When her youngest son Billy passed due to brain cancer, her world stopped. This is where the book starts. The communication with him helped to get her through that tough time. There are many beautiful, comforting, and surprising messages from him in the book.

If you want to contact Ruthe Ann, the email is: RAWartist@aol.com

She also has a page on Facebook: ShoreThingJewels. There will be prints of some of the artwork available.

Books and People I recommend:

The Heart of Healing: Discovering the Secrets of Self-Care. By Regina Rosenthal, PT, MA. Treatments with Regina were very helpful and she would receive messages from Billy during them.

Celestial Conversations–Healing Relationships After Death. By Lo Anne Mayer. It was so good to read this book and the next one as well, to know other people had this happen to them and I was not going crazy. (LOL)

The Afterlife of Billy Fingers by Annie Kagan.

Seasons Change and So Do I. By Carol Vigoda Fuchs. This is a wonderful children's book to help them deal with loss.

Brigitta Boyea, Light Bridge, Inc.   http://lightbridge101.com
She was very helpful in getting me started with communication between my son and me.

CPSIA information can be obtained
at www.ICGtesting.com
Printed in the USA
BVHW021521041221
623049BV00001B/4